DEDICATION

To
Sandra and Bill for their seemingly endless
generosity and kindness

ISBN 1 899417 00 1

Published by:
Panna Dipa Books
6 Brighton Terrace, Douglas, Isle of Man, IM1 4AP.
Tel: 01624 612819

Printed by:
Nelson Press Co. Ltd.
Kingswood Grove, Douglas, Isle of Man, IM1 3LY.

CONTENTS

1.   IT'S IN NO SPECIAL PLACE

2.   EVERYTHING IS PRACTICE

3.   SWEEPING THE LEAVES

4.   MAGIC OR WISDOM?

5.   NOT TODAY

6.   DON'T DEFEND YOURSELF

7.   LOOKING AT OURSELVES

8.   LOVE OPENLY

9.   KEEP IT SIMPLE

10. THE EMPTY MIND

11. LIVING IN THE SUNSHINE

12. NO-ONE CAN DO IT FOR YOU

13. HIGHER THAN HAPPINESS

EVERYTHING IS PRACTICE

A young physician went to a Zen Master and asked to be taught Zen.

"Zen is not such a difficult practice," said the Master. "If you are a physician, treat your patients with kindness, that is Zen."

The physician visited the Master three times, but on each occasion he was told the same thing. The Master said, "A physician should not waste his time here, go home and look after your patients."

It was not clear how such a teaching could remove the doubts and confusion about life that the physician had, and so on the fourth visit he complained to the Master.

The Master smiled and said, "Perhaps I have been too hard on you. I will give you a meditation to practice." He instructed the physician in Insight meditation.

The physician practised this form of meditation each day for two years. At length he thought he had attained clarity of mind, but the Master commented, "You are not there yet."

The physician continued to practice. In time his mind became calm and balanced. Problems and doubt dissolved. Emptiness became the Truth. He served his patients well, and without ever knowing it, became free from the concern over life and death.

The next time he visited the Master, the Master simply smiled.

It is a recurrent theme of mine that spiritual life is ordinary life. There is no separation between the two. To progress in spiritual understanding there is no need to renounce the world, to give up the ordinary things of life and lock yourself away in a cave or a monastery. To cut yourself off from the world. There is no requirement to become a monk or a nun or a recluse. Living in the world is excellent practice.

For many years I worked in a factory alongside six hundred others.

Factory life is difficult for many people, and does seem to encourage the lowest aspects of mind. It is the same with all work that seems pointless and empty. Pettiness, mental dullness and irritation are common. So is back biting, tale bearing and gossip. However, these are the things that fill the day, and break the most overpowering mental state of all, that of boredom. Boredom with the work, boredom with the people, and boredom with life. I rarely met people enthusiastic about their job.

To find yourself in a situation like this can be very testing, soul destroying in fact, but in spiritual training we must remember that everything depends upon attitude.

If you are doing something you don't want to do, then everything connected with it becomes a drudge. Having to work in such conditions can seem like a prison sentence, but if you see this as an opportunity to train and develop, then everything changes for you. No more drudge, just the chance to practice.

When things go well, there is the moment for you to see your mind and watch your reactions. When things do not go well, there is the same opportunity. It all depends on attitude.

Do you see this as the chance to practice or not?

If you say yes, there are no more problems for you. Everything changes. However, if you say no, right there in that answer, is the arising of unhappiness.

Unhappiness begins in the mind of the person who always wants everything to go his, or her own way.

I was very fortunate in my time at the factory. I would begin each day with meditation, go to work, meditate at lunch time, continue work, go home and meditate again. I had formal meditation and working meditation. What an opportunity to practice. Being with so many people, all very different to me, was the chance to watch myself. To watch my mind.

On reflection I value my time at the factory very much. I learnt a lot about myself, my ego and how it manifests, and most importantly, how to surrender. When there is no choice, the only thing to do is surrender, to be open and learn.

We cannot always choose the conditions we live under. No matter how hard we try, we are not able to make everything perfect according to our desires, and as long as we attempt to do this, we will suffer.

Look at the world. Look how everyone follows this path, and look at the results when they fail. Misery, anger and unhappiness.

From the position of practice, everything is perfect just as it is. There are no special conditions we have to create. Nothing special we have to do. Whether we work in a factory, a shop, an office, or stay at home and look after the house and family, right there are the perfect conditions for practice. There is nothing outside your mind and body, and so nothing is outside your practice.

Let go of the desire to make everything the way you think it should be, and be with things as they are. Look at your mind, your feelings, your reactions, and there is your practice. Learn to be open and accepting. This is the practice of the enlightened mind. The free mind. Choosing one thing over another is the foundation of unhappiness. Let go of choice and be with what is.

In life we all have to experience many different conditions, some good, some not so good, some downright painful. All of us are subject to the whole range of human emotions and feelings. It is the same for everyone. Pleasure and pain arise endlessly, and as long as we are attached to one over the other, we will suffer.
One Zen Master has said, 'The Way is simple, it just means giving up picking and choosing.'
Usually we would all prefer pleasant bodily sensation to unpleasant bodily sensation, pain, but the story of the meditation teacher in hospital might help us let go even of this choice.

He had awoken at home in the early morning with severe pain in his abdomen. This became increasingly worse as the morning progressed, and finally a doctor was called. The doctor suspected kidney stones, and so sent him to hospital for an examination. Once in the hospital, still waiting to be seen, and the pain intensifying each minute, the meditation teacher, in a moment of desperation, heard himself exclaim, 'Jesus Christ, take this pain away.'
Then, from somewhere in the back of his mind a voice replied, 'Take it away, I've only just given it to you.'

Everything is the opportunity to practice, the painful experiences as well as the pleasant. Learn to look at your life as a gift, the chance to attain full enlightenment. The end of all your suffering and unhappiness, and cultivate a mind that will use every possible opportunity to achieve it.

SWEEPING THE LEAVES

Everything we experience happens within our mind

SWEEPING THE LEAVES

At one time a young monk was asked to look after an old, almost derelict temple in the hills in Japan. He felt pleased to do this as his nature was to be precise in his actions, and this would be the opportunity for him to make something from nothing. To renovate an old building and to have it just the way he wanted it to be.

Living alongside the Temple was an enlightened Master. He had retired from teaching and enjoyed the peace of a quiet life. One of the young monks duties was to look after the Master, to prepare his food and attend to his needs.

One day a message was received that the young monk was to expect a visit from his superiors, who would assess the work he had done on the temple. All morning he worked hard, cleaning and preparing for the visit. He wanted everywhere to look as good as it could. Finally there was just one job left.

The night before there had been a strong wind, and the garden was strewn with leaves that had blown down from the tree standing in the centre of the lawn. The young monk took his wooden broom and began to sweep. Carefully gathering the fallen leaves together, he put them in a sack and removed them from the garden, all the while watched by the Master who was leaning on the adjoining fence. When the very last leaf had been carried away, the young monk turned to the Master and asked him what he thought.

"Not bad, not bad," said the Master, "There is just one thing needed to make it perfect."

The young monk was hesitant. He had done everything he could think of. What more could there be?

"Just help me over the fence and I'll show you," continued the Master.

Reluctantly the young monk obeyed. He had come to

know this Master, and knew to expect the unexpected. The Master, once in the temple grounds, staggered over to the tree in the centre of the garden, and with all the strength in his frail old body, shook it as hard as he could. The remaining leaves fluttered down onto the lawn, falling into a haphazard pattern. As the young monks superiors could be seen climbing the hill to the temple, the Master turned to him and said, "Now, everything's perfect."

We all have a perception of perfection. We carry with us an idea of how everything should be, and because of this, spend huge amounts of time and energy trying to arrange conditions to match this idea. Our family, friends, partners and colleagues, our work and social engagements. Nothing falls outside our desire to be happy by controlling all the things we think we need to produce that happiness. It is a constant struggle.

The blueprint for perfection against the realities of life.

However, perfection as it is usually understood, is just an idea. It is a concept, and not only can it not be realised in any real and lasting way, our perception of it is always changing anyway.

What made us happy once may not have the same effect a second time, and so we change our requirements. Our mind is always moving. Thoughts, feelings, moods and emotions, come and go without end, and so, what was necessary in any particular moment to fulfil our concept of perfection is always changing and adjusting itself to fit our needs and desires.

And even if we do manage to contrive a situation when everything seems perfect, there is always something that interferes with it. A 'phone call when we finally manage to sink into a hot bath at the end of a long hard day, or the need to get up and make a cup of tea when we're relaxing, or simply having to go to the toilet in the middle of our favourite television programme.

The perfect state, even if it can be touched, is fleeting.

Meditation practice can be like this. Trying to arrange circumstances so that they are perfect for us. A time when we can be alone, in comfortable surroundings, and not be disturbed. Then we can really get on with our practice. Then we can really watch the mind.

But the mind that we see in meditation is not a special mind. It is not something that only appears when we sit quietly. It is the mind that is always with us. Sitting quietly or not, it comes and goes by itself, filled with thoughts, distractions, pleasant feelings and unpleasant feelings.

And the desire to make everything perfect.

If we are dedicated to self investigation, we have to realise that whether we are sitting in meditation or not, this awareness practice can still continue. Physical posture, in the end, counts for very little. Awareness is everything. To notice the nature of the mind, and to be at peace with it, is the fruit of practice. Not constantly seeking to fulfil an idea of how everything should be, but being at peace with things as they are, creates perfect practice.

Of course, this attitude demands something from us. It demands surrender.

In common usage surrender means reluctantly giving up something we really want. We feel the need to hold onto a particular object, an idea, a feeling or an emotion, and because of circumstances beyond our control, it is being taken away from us. Like soldiers on a battle field. When the bullets have all been fired, there is no choice but to give in. To surrender.

However, in spiritual terms surrender means something different. It means to let go. To be in harmony. To give up the struggle with life, and to be easy. Making choices and decisions when they are available, but not suffering when we have to accept circumstances we cannot change. Surrender means to be centred. To be in control of our life. Real control. Not of the external, but the internal. Of our responses and reactions.

Everything we experience happens within our mind. Anger, fear, frustration, and all our negative mental states, begin and end within us. No-one gives them to us, and no-one can take them away. We do it to ourselves. As we begin to understand this, we can peacefully let them go. Not attempting to drive them away with an attitude of, 'I shouldn't feel like this', but to see them for what they are. Impersonal movements of mind, not me, not mine, not what I am. They are like visitors to your house. Perhaps you don't like them, but you can still be kind and polite. You don't have to ask them to stay, but you don't need to throw them out either. Eventually, and without any fuss, they will grow tired and leave by themselves.

Happiness is the same. It begins and ends within us. No-one gives it to us, and no-one can take it away. But if we feel we are dependent upon certain circumstances for our happiness, then it can always be lost. Someone or something can take it away from us. This type of happiness, established in our quest for perfection, is truly superficial and naturally has no sustaining power.

If someone can give it, then someone can always take it away again.

True happiness comes from Dhamma. If peace and

acceptance are our starting points, then everything else flows. Whatever the circumstances, we can be happy. Not trying to create a world where everything is the way we think it should be, but being at peace with things as they are.

No fight. No struggle.

The leaves falling from the tree is not the problem. Seeing them on the ground and wishing they were not there is the problem. Whether others see things our way or not, is not the problem, feeling the need to make them do so is the problem.

Open your heart through practice. Let go of the desire to create a perfect world for yourself, and be easy. Perfection is only an idea anyway. It only truly exists when we see that everything is already perfect, just as it is.

MAGIC OR WISDOM?

**If we want to remove unhappiness from our lives
we have to remove ignorance**

MAGIC OR WISDOM?

Once when a Zen Master was preaching at a certain temple, a follower from another tradition, who was in the audience, was causing a disturbance. Because he was jealous of the Masters reputation, he sought to discredit him by engaging in a debate.

The Master eventually invited the man to the front of the crowd and allowed him to speak.

"The founder of our sect has such miraculous powers," began the man, "That if he stood on one bank of a river and drew letters in the air, they would appear on a piece of paper held by an attendant on the other bank. Can you do such a wonderful thing?"

"Perhaps your fox can perform that sort of magic," said the Zen Master, "But that is not the way of Zen. My magic is that when I eat, I really eat, and when I drink, I really drink."

There is a common fascination with magic and the attainment of miraculous powers. Many people involve themselves in so called 'spiritual practice', for just such reasons. The development of special powers, such as magic and healing, sets one apart from others, and is generally understood as being synonymous with spiritual progress. However, for other spiritual practitioners, the acquisition of magical powers can actually be seen as a hindrance. An obstacle to the truth.

The reality is to be more balanced, relaxed and open. If they occur naturally, all well and good, but if one actively seeks them, look at your motives. Who exactly wants what?

I, myself, many years ago, before discovering meditation,

became very interested in Astral Projection. I was fascinated by the idea that one could leave ones own body and not only travel in this world, but also visit other planes of existence. I bought and read many books on the subject, and spent perhaps hundreds of hours practising the exercises and techniques I had read. All to no avail. I never went anywhere, and eventually I gave up trying.
But I was interested - for a while.

Actually it's not surprising that people from our cultures have this specific interest in magic when you remember Jesus and the Bible stories. The miracles form an important part of the Christian belief system, and to most people, are what Jesus is actually remembered for. Turning water into wine, walking on the water, and raising the dead. The teaching itself comes second to the miracles, which are seen as the proof of the divinity of Christ.

There was once a Master telling a story to a student to curb his interest in acquiring magical powers. The story was about another teacher who wanted to cross a river. He approached the boatman and asked him to ferry him across.
"That will cost you one penny," said the boatman.
"But I don't have a penny," replied the teacher.
"Then I won't take you across," said the boatman.
On hearing those words the teacher stepped off the bank of the river and walked across on the water.

The Master who was telling the story explained to his student that such a trick is not even worth the penny he should have paid to the boatman in the first place.
Such is a Masters understanding of the value of magic.

Although magic can be impressive, it does not necessarily indicate wisdom, and it is only wisdom that will save ourselves and the world we live in. As long as there is no wisdom, there is an abundance of ignorance, and ignorance always means confusion, both for ourselves and others. Couple that with magical powers and there can really be a dangerous situation. Ego, that part of us that needs to be seen as someone special, someone different from the crowd, can lead us to act in a way that will bring only harm, no matter how noble or pure minded we think our actions are. As long as there is ego, there is always the danger of abuse.

So what is to be done?

All spiritual traditions speak of magic, but all Masters dismiss it as irrelevant. It's just not important. It's not an indication of anything.
The real magic in spiritual practice is the intuitive understanding of mind and body. Of knowing ourselves by realising the nature of our reality. Of being balanced and at peace, whatever is happening.

There is another story of a Zen Master whose monastery was being attacked by an invading force. The Master sat in meditation, untroubled by what was happening, until he was at last disturbed by the leader of the attackers who placed a sword at his throat and said, "I am one who can run you through without batting an eyelid."
"And I sir," replied the Zen Master, "Am one who can be run through without batting an eyelid."
This is real magic. Complete equanimity, established in a deep experience and understanding of reality. How could this man ever be defeated?

As one turns inward more and more through the development of a calm and peaceful mind, ones abilities naturally develop.

All of us can recognise anger in another. It's not usually very difficult to see, even if that person is actively trying not to show it. Always something, some gesture or phrase betrays them. However, from the meditative mind, our abilities to recognise even the most subtle mental states of others becomes greatly sharpened, as we ourselves become more sensitive and less ego based.

Less outward projection into the world, and more balance.

Perhaps you would call this 'mind reading', a magical power, but in reality it is just an opening of ourselves. Being receptive to the minds of others, without enforcing our will onto a situation.

We have to understand that the cause of our unhappiness, however we define it, is ourselves, and nothing, not even the attainment of magical powers will alter that.

The whole of the Buddhas teaching revolves around this point. All of our unhappiness and struggle with life is caused by desire and craving, wanting things to be other than they are, and these have their roots in ignorance. If we want to remove unhappiness from our lives, we have to remove ignorance. Nothing else will do it.

Nothing.

The central theme of true spiritual training is removing ignorance, of knowing the mind and body as they really are, and not trying to develop special powers. It is our continual identification with the delusion of self that causes all our problems, and not even being able to walk on water or through walls, will change this.

The real magic is in wisdom, and real power lies in non-attachment to the mind and body complex, we call self. If you truly want to develop yourself, develop in the way of wisdom. Wisdom leads to peace and happiness, and from that, everyone benefits.

The Master in the story at the beginning knew where real power lay. Not in magical tricks and displays, but in simply being with the ordinary things in life. In giving full attention to the acts of eating and drinking, and everything else he was involved in. This is real ability, and will without doubt, lead to the overcoming of sorrow and unhappiness, and the desire to be someone special.
It will lead to the realisation of the Truth, and the complete knowing of oneself.

NOT TODAY

Death will occur, and we don't know when

NOT TODAY

There was once a flock of sheep who lived in a meadow. One day a rumour began that the farmer was going to kill them all, so one sheep was elected to pay the farmer a visit and ask him if this was true.

After some time the sheep returned to the meadow skipping and hopping and smiling broadly.

"Well," said the rest of the flock, "Is he going to kill us?"

"Yes," replied the sheep, "But not today."

It is true that death faces us all. It is inescapable.

From the moment we are born it is the only thing we can know with any real certainty, and as much as we may want things to be otherwise, it is completely beyond our control.

We can do many things to improve the quality of our life, such as exercise, eating good foods and even involving ourselves in a meditation practice, but at some point all this must end. Death will come no matter what we do. No-one can live forever, and everyone who is born has to die.

I have heard that in Ireland there are a group of people who believe that death is conditioned solely by thinking about it, and if it is never thought about, or brought up in conversation, it just won't happen. This is their philosophy, and if it turns out to be true, and they don't die, they will be the first people ever to live and not have to face their own death.

Even enlightened beings have had to die. The Buddha died at eighty, Jesus at thirty three. Even Methusala in the Bible had to die. He lived until he was seven hundred years old, but in one moment it was over. Death occurred, and nothing more could be done.

And it can happen at any time. Look around you.
People die young. Babies die, children die, adolescents and young adults die. It is not only the old that have to face death. From the moment we are born it is the only sure thing in life. Death will occur, and we don't know when.

But not today.

At least, not in this moment.

In this moment we are alive.

Right now we have life, and right now we have the best possible opportunity of living it to the full. Of making the most of every second there is.

Of course, in spiritual terms, living life to the full does not mean going to parties, drinking alcohol or taking other drugs. It does not mean using other people for our own advantage, sexually or otherwise, or taking objects that belong to them.
It means seizing every moment as an opportunity to develop in wisdom.

Life is so precious, that not to use it in this way is simply a waste.

As we deepen the understanding of ourselves through the practice of Insight and Loving Kindness Meditation, we begin to see and appreciate the value of life. Our past habits and conditioning become revealed to us, and allowed to fall away. The resultant clarity of the now spacious mind provides the condition for the experience of life to be understood fully.

Not to use others, but to be of use. Not to harm others, but to be gentle and kind. Not to be confused by the appearance of things, but to use every moment to allow the Truth to arise within us. This is how we can learn to live to our limitless limit.
To live life to the full.

Unpleasant mental states come and go by themselves. So do the pleasant ones, like clouds passing through a clear blue sky. Not me, not mine, not what I am.

Only mind moving.

The more we are able to experience this simple truth with loving awareness, the more complete will be our liberation from the trap of the mind.
When we are free from this trap, we are free even from the thought of life and death.

One teacher has said, 'No-one was ever born, and no-one will ever die.'
If we can understand this truth fully, not with the intellect, but with the intuitive mind, the Spiritual Heart, we are liberated forever from the distinction between life and death.

So when you are alive, live.

Don't waste a moment. Don't die before you learn how to make the most of this precious time.

This is the opportunity of life.

Many people ask me, 'What is the purpose of life?' and I always give the same reply. 'There is no purpose to life.'

There is no cosmic scheme behind our existence. No being directing us or ordaining certain events for us. Everything is entirely in our own hands. Life, as we experience it, is a consequence. It is a result of something that has gone before.

There is no inherent purpose to life, but it is an opportunity. It is the opportunity of liberation. Only humans can realise enlightenment. The gods, or so called 'higher beings', can't do it, and neither can the beings in the animal kingdom. Only humans have the opportunity and capability to fully know themselves and so be liberated from the realms of suffering and unhappiness.

Right now you have this opportunity. What will you do with it?

To say, "Oh, I'll start tomorrow," may be leaving it too late, and next year, or even next week may never come for you.

Don't allow this chance to slip by. Only you can cultivate your life so that it becomes a blessing for yourself and the world.
As beautiful as a lotus growing in a muddy pool.

Death will come to you, that is for sure.

But not today.

Don't miss this moment.

DON'T DEFEND YOURSELF

Conforming makes everyones life more comfortable

DON'T DEFEND YOURSELF

Zen students take a vow that even if they are killed by their teacher, their intention is to truly learn Zen. This has now become just a formality, and is usually declared by the cutting of a finger. However, in olden times it was a completely different matter.

Eikido had become a stern master, and all his students feared him. One day a student striking a gong to tell the time of day, missed a beat when his eye was attracted by a beautiful girl passing by the temple gate. At that moment Eikido, who was standing directly behind him, hit him on the head with his stick. The shock of the blow killed the student outright.

The guardian of the the dead boy, hearing of the incident, went immediately to Eikido. Knowing he was not to blame, he praised the master for his severe teaching. Eikido's attitude was just the same as if the student were still alive.

After this took place Eikido was able to produce more than ten enlightened successors, a very unusual number.

Our usual way of being is to live in accordance with the rules and regulations set down by others. To play other peoples games. They tell us what is right and what is wrong, and most importantly, how we should behave. This is simply conditioning by our parents, our educational system and society in general. At a very early age we learn that certain modes of behaviour are either acceptable or not. We loose spontaneous action because in our mind we are always trapped by this conditioning.

A friend of mine 'phoned me one day to ask a question.

She had been in a relationship with a man, which had ended, and was now seeing someone else. The first man had met her unexpectedly one day and expressed the desire to rekindle their involvement with each other. However, there was a condition. She had to stop seeing the other man. He told her that she must choose. One or the other.

My friend was confused. She liked them both. What should she do?

I told her that she didn't have to do anything. Making a choice between the two men in her life was someone elses game, and she didn't have to play. If she wanted to see one, or the other, or neither or both, that was a choice that she could make.

There was no need for her to feel forced into a situation by the demands of someone else. She was free to make her own decision. To live her own life.

This is how it is for most of us. We find ourselves dragged into playing other peoples games. Even if we don't want to, because of our past conditioning, we find it hard to resist, and therefore live our life according to the demands of others. We never fully experience a sense of freedom because of continual external pressure from parents, friends, family and the rest of society. They all know how we should be, and if we resist their view of life, they turn up the pressure.

Conforming makes everyones life more comfortable.

To live a spiritual life means to stop playing this game. To be your own person.

It does not mean however, that we just become more selfish and self centred, completely disregarding the feelings of others. On the contrary, through the investigation of mind and body, we develop, and then continue to develop, a less selfish view of ourselves and the world we live in. We become more open and harmonious to the feelings of others. But, from the position of selflessness and balance, we can see impartially what needs to be done, and what needs to be left undone. We are no longer swayed by opinion. We do what is right to do.

In order to reach this state of being we have to let go of our ego, and the need to see ourselves, and be seen by others in a certain light. To continually reinforce the idea that we are nice people, and therefore only capable of good actions. We have to learn to be open to ourselves, however we are. With this comes confidence, not conceit. Not the idea that only we know what is best for everyone, but the knowledge that each must make their way in the world as they see fit. We can help of course, be of service, but never be compromised by the opinion of others.
This means that what others think of us means nothing.
Everyone is criticised from time to time. Look at the lives of Jesus and the Buddha. Both were enlightened, but both were subject to many criticisms from the unenlightened. However, the opinions of others did not concern them. Their only concern was the Truth, and how to express it best.

When we embark upon a spiritual life we have to develop purity. This is what a spiritual life means, a pure life. At the beginning we may need to follow certain rules of training, guidelines that will help us cultivate that purity.
These rules are fundamental to progress along the spiritual path, and discourage killing, or inflicting pain on other beings, stealing, using our speech in wrong and harmful ways, sexual misconduct and the use of drinks and drugs that tend to cloud the mind.

But these guidelines should not be seen as acts of repression. We have to investigate and understand the outcome of such acts, and realise that not only do the victims suffer, but that we also suffer. All breaches of morality stem from ego, from the desire to create and maintain perfect conditions of life for ourselves. It is exactly this reasoning we have to let go of.

Our morality must be a natural morality, coming from a pure heart, a pure centre. This can only happen when our intention is to train ourselves in the way of an enlightened being. It is said that the moral training of the Buddhist is simply the way an enlightened being behaves in the world. We act as though we are already enlightened, in harmony with all beings.

When I was in India, staying in the small town of Banda, I was asked about killing mosquitoes. Now I, like everyone else, do not like mosquitoes very much. I don't like them on me, and I certainly don't like them to bite me. However, the desire to kill them simply does not arise. I will blow them off, or gently brush them off with my hand, but in my heart I wish them no harm.

To live in harmony with even the things we don't like is truly a blessing, both for ourselves and all other beings.

When we act from purity the need to defend or explain our actions does not arise. If there is no self, no ego performing, who is there to explain anything?

It is the ego, the delusion that we are someone and something, that needs to be defended, and can always justify every deed we do.

It is the ego that needs to be accepted by others, praised and given a pat on the back. When this aspect of us acts, it is always with an ulterior motive. Self promotion.

Now try this experiment for a week. Don't defend yourself.
If you do something wrong, apologise, and let it go. Don't attempt to justify or explain it. Don't demand that others see your point of view.
Just let it go. Don't feed the ego.

When Ananda, the Buddhas cousin and attendant for twenty five years was accused of wrong conduct, he simply answered his accusers by saying, 'In my heart I did no wrong, but if you say I did, then I apologise.'

No explanation, no justification, no defence. Only an answer coming from the purity of being.

And if you perform an act of kindness, keep quiet, Again, there is no need to explain why you did what you did. It's done, gone, finished. Let it go.

The purpose of spiritual training is to assist the forces of ego and conceit to die out, and to allow the pure mind to manifest. This mind simply is. When this mind is present, where are you? Where is ego?
Pure mind and ego are like light and darkness. They cannot exist together. When pure mind isn't present, there you are, with all your views, opinions, belief and conceit. A bundle of delusion making its way in the world, causing chaos for all concerned.

Every moment we are awake is a moment to be. A moment to let this pure mind manifest by not allowing the influences of ego and self preservation come to the fore.
When the mind pulls in the direction of ego, simply see it

for what it is, and let it go. You're not your mind, and you're not your body. There is nothing that you really are, and no mould you have to fit.

Be yourself. Act from the position of egolessness.

Set yourself free.

LOOKING AT OURSELVES

What place can hide us from ourselves?

LOOKING AT OURSELVES

After a famous meditation teacher had passed away, a blind man who lived close to the monastery told a friend, "Since I am blind, I cannot watch a persons face so I must judge his character by the sound of his voice. Usually when I hear someone congratulate another upon his happiness or success, I also hear a secret tone of envy or jealousy. Also, when I hear condolence for the misfortune of another, I hear pleasure or a faint trace of satisfaction in that persons voice. However, in all my experience with the Master, his voice was always sincere. Whenever he expressed happiness, I heard nothing but happiness, and when he expressed sorrow, sorrow was all I heard."

At the very heart of spiritual practice is meditation, the turning away from the world of ego and the senses, and the investigation of mind and body. The foundation of who and what we think we are. This investigation can go on for many lifetimes as the veneers of ego and conceit are slowly eroded, and our true nature revealed. The method of meditation we use in this investigation is Insight Meditation. It is the only way to truly see and know ourselves as we really are.

In this form of meditation nothing is hidden, for the very object of our attention is only our own mind and body. What place can hide us from ourselves?

All our fears, doubts, desires and delusions are revealed in an atmosphere of calm and balanced observation. Eventually nothing will escape our detached watchfulness. But to do this we need to be brave. We need to go deep into the heart of our delusion of who and what we think we are.

No matter how honest we believe ourselves to be, our usual

everyday mind has created an image of ourself that is untrue.

We may think that we are kind and generous people, always willing to help others, and be of service, but the reality is something other than that.

Conversely, we may believe that we are low and unworthy, not good enough for the trust and friendship of others, but this too is not true.

Whatever view we hold about ourselves is just a view. It is not the truth.

Because of our basic delusion as to how we regard ourselves, we all suffer from the same condition, that of ego, that part of us which believes itself to be real and lasting. To be a definite force in the world, for better or worse. It is this part that holds all its own views and opinions, and of course, always believes them to be the best.

It is this part that does not want to die, or be got rid of, and for that very reason, can be very devious. It knows every level of subtlety and deceit. It can fool others, but more importantly, it can fool us. This ego has been around for a very long time, gathering strength and vitality, always waiting for an opportunity to assert itself.

We believe we were something in the past, and that we will be something in the future. When ego arises, a history arises, and when that history arises, the whole delusion of who and what we are arises. Without investigation, attachment to the ego will never be broken. We will never be free from its influence, and the unhappiness it inevitably brings.

This ego is always out for itself. It is always after a prize, a reward, sometimes large, sometimes small, but always something. Perhaps it is something as subtle as simply feeling good after performing a kindness, or just needing a 'thank you', for a gift, or work done, but whatever it is, it always needs something for itself from every situation. Always.

Generally speaking, we like to think of ourselves in a favourable light. A person of integrity and substance. Someone worthy of the respect and approval of others. In short, an all round nice person. Even when we do perform an unwholesome act, and suffer the pricks of conscience, we can usually justify our action, and put it behind us. Onward, onward to the future, carrying all of our past habits and conditioning with us.
Because of ego we are self centred and always self motivated.
This is how it is for all of us.

Ego is the manifestation of ignorance.

Insight Meditation is not only the investigation of this process, but also the breaking of it.
By recognising ego as the cause of our unhappiness we can make the decision not to feed it any more. Not to indulge in its fantasies, and so take away its power. The Buddha has said that the best way to put out a fire is simply not to add any more fuel to it. To let it burn itself out. Ego is the fire within us.
However, once we begin this process of no longer feeding the ego, we have to allow the stockpile of conceit and confusion, accumulated in the past, rise up from our subconscious, and let it go. Let everything go. We have to

give up any views of who and what we think we are, and be open to whatever arises.

This means to no longer identify ourselves as a particular type of person, who should think or act in a certain way. These views are just conditioning, indoctrinated into us by our parents, friends, peers and the rest of society in general. There are no set patterns we have to adhere to.

To think that we should never have horrible thoughts will only create problems for us, because when we lift the lid off this dustbin of our mind, be sure, they will be there.

Our habits and conditioning arise from the past to confront us now, in the present. They are inescapable. In order not to fuel them for the future, we have to see them for what they really are, mental states arising because of conditions. Not me, not mine, not what I am.

Our mind stream flows on and on, every thought experienced now affecting it and conditioning it for the future. This is the process we have to break.

Ego is not a problem. To think of ourselves as good, or to think of ourselves as bad or unworthy, is merely the opportunity to train. To see ourselves as we really are. Simply a mass of ever changing moods, thoughts, feelings and emotions, affecting the accumulation of matter we call body. Nothing more than that. There is no underlying 'Self' that we really are. No cosmic soul or entity that is in any way worthy of praise or blame. Just process. The whole of our existence is just process. An activity of becoming, that never becomes anything.

This is what we have to investigate.

The ego is without substance. The 'Self', or soul is without substance. Nothing was ever born, and nothing will ever

56

die, but as long as we are attached to mind and body, the delusion of 'Self', it will always appear that way.

Insight Meditation only investigates this delusion. The delusion of 'Self'. It doesn't say it is real, and it doesn't say it is not real. It says 'look for yourself, what do you see?' Pleasant thoughts come and go by themselves. So do the unpleasant ones. Nothing lasts for more than a moment, and everything is part of this changing process.

Give up your identification with your habitual thought patterns, see what you really are, and what you really are not.

You're not your body, and you're not your mind.

Be free.

LOVE OPENLY

**When we know where to look for the truth,
all our problems and judgements fall away**

LOVE OPENLY

There was once a nun who went to train at an exclusively male monastery. She was very disciplined in her practice, and also very beautiful. Because of this many of the monks quickly fell in love with her. One monk was so overwhelmed by her beauty that he could not resist writing her a note. The note said, 'I love you very much. Meet me in the garden after evening meditation.' As she walked past he handed it to her.

When the meditation had finished she read the note and stood up. Facing the monk who had written it she said, "If you truly love me so much, come here and embrace me now."

The monk just hung his head in shame.

In Dhamma terms we say, 'If you love, love openly'.

This simply means to be honest with our feelings and motivations. To be sincere. But in the world, this is not how we live. So many games being played, so many people looking for their own share of happiness. So much confusion, and so much pain.

Everyone wants to be happy of course, and for most of us this includes an intimate relationship with another person. Someone we can share our life with. Someone we can grow with. Someone we can love. However, our expectations of our partner can be very high indeed, and often the feeling arises that they have failed us in some way. Perhaps they are irritable in the mornings, or they won't help around the house, or they are just not good at dealing with the finances, but our response is to believe that they have let us down in some way, and we feel that the one person we had pinned all our hopes of happiness on to is in fact, not the one for us. Perhaps we need to find someone else. Someone else who can make us happy.

One young girl asked me if I knew of any way to make her boyfriend jealous. When I asked why she would want to do such a thing, she replied, 'Because I want him to marry me.'
This is a very dangerous game to play, and one would have to question her motivation. In any case, it would seem unlikely that such a relationship could be happy in the long term if it was established on such an unwholesome mental state as jealousy.

It is true that when we don't know the nature of our mind, we don't look at the outcome of what we do. Because of our confusion, we create certain monsters and set them free. We hope for the best, but they always come back to hurt us. Always.

To love openly means to be free from self centred motivation, and to give love. To be accepting of other people, and respect them. Even if they are doing things we think they should not do. Even if they behave in a way we don't approve of. Even if they hurt us.
In worldly relationships we always work on the other person, trying to mould them to suit ourselves. In a Dhamma relationship we work on ourself. Checking our motivation, and looking at the result of our action. If our motivation is pure, then whatever happens, we are blameless. We don't have to make excuses, and we don't have to find someone else to blame either.

A Dhamma life means a pure life. It is a gradual growth from ego to egolessness. A movement from darkness to light. Along this path there will be many problems and difficulties, but if we keep our motivation pure, the outcome will always be beneficial.

When we no longer live in the world acting only upon our selfish desires and habits, we demonstrate love. It's truly that simple.

Love is not something we need to cultivate and develop, it is a quality we already have. When we don't have an ego based self directing everything we do, love manifests.
This is to love openly. Not in secret, not with shame, not with an ulterior motive or the fear that someone may find out exactly what we are doing, but with an openess established in pure motivation.

It is the practice of letting go.

When we judge others and complain about their actions, we are always looking outside ourselves. We are missing the point of Insight training. Insight training means to look at the mind that is actually making those judgements, and not the objects of them. It means to have a clear picture of what is really happening, and where it is happening. Not outside. Not in the world. But in our own mind. Only in our mind.
When we know where to look for the truth, all our problems and judgements fall away.

One meditation Master has said, 'No-one ever became wise through criticising others.'

Wisdom only arises when we look at ourselves, at our ego, and our selfish desire for personal happiness, and see it for what it really is. An impersonal movement of mind. Not me, not mine, not what I really am.

The qualities we think we want, such as kindness, compassion, tolerance and love, just be them.
Be what you really are. Don't let ego get in the way. Life is too precious for that.

So in your life, be happy. In your meditation, go deep. And in your love, give it freely. Love openly and without conditions. Love is too beautiful, too valuable to be part of the barter system of life. It is something we need to give freely and without expectation of something in return.
'I will love you if you love me back', is not love. It is a trade. It is a businessman's love. It cannot ever be beautiful, and so cannot ever be sustained. It is only a game.

Let your need for love be overwhelmed by your desireless desire to give love. Let your spiritual heart transform your emotional heart, and let your pain and suffering fall away into the emptiness of the universe.

KEEP IT SIMPLE

Spiritual Life is essentially a simple affair

KEEP IT SIMPLE

There was once a Master called Kitano Gempo. The whole of his training was devoted to the breaking of attachment. When he was twenty, and living as a wandering mendicant, he met a fellow traveller who smoked tobacco. As they rested one day the traveller offered Kitano a smoke, which he accepted as he was very hungry at the time.

Kitano enjoyed the smoke, and when he and the traveller parted, he was given the gift of a pipe and some tobacco. Soon however, he realised how attracted he was becoming to smoking, so he gave it up. 'This tobacco is very pleasant, and such pleasant things may disturb my meditation,' he thought.

Later in life he found himself having to endure a cold and hard winter. He wrote a letter to his Master asking for some warm clothes. They never arrived. Knowing that his Master would not deliberately ignore his plight, he decided to find out whether his letter had been received or not. To do this he consulted the 'I Ching', the ancient Chinese book of divination. The results could not be disputed. The letter had not been received. This fact was later confirmed by a message from his Master, making no mention of his request for warm clothes. 'If I perform such accurate work with the 'I Ching', I may neglect my meditation,' thought Kitano, and so he gave it up. He never consulted it again.

As he grew older he studied Chinese calligraphy and poetry. He became so skilful in these arts that even his teachers praised him. Once again Kitano saw these merely as distractions to his meditation. 'If I don't stop now I will become a poet, not a Master of Zen,' and so immediately stopped.

He never wrote another poem again.

Spiritual life is essentially a simple affair. To progress in it means to watch your attachments fall away until you are left with purity of being.

Selflessness.

Ordinary life is just the opposite. Holding onto more and more things. Material objects, favourite possessions, memories, opinions and ideas. Identification with our mind and body. To realise our spiritual potential we must break our attachments. We must give up clinging.

However this may sound, it doesn't actually mean we have to give everything away, or no longer hold any views and opinions, it means we have to break our attachment to them. We have to see them for what they are.

Often we hear it said that 'Money is the root of all evil', but this is not correct. The complete expression is, 'The love of money is the root of all evil'. Money is fine. Money itself is completely neutral. It is our love of money, or our attachment to it, that causes all the problems.

At one time the Buddha was asked where suffering and unhappiness begins. He answered, 'Suffering and unhappiness begin in love and attachment.'

The person asking the question was a king, and was not happy with the answer, so the Buddha explained.

'Your Majesty, suppose your son was kidnapped and held for ransom, with threats of murder if you didn't comply with the demands of the kidnappers. How would you feel?'

'Devastated,' said the king, 'My life would be in turmoil, and I would do anything to ensure the safe return of my son.'

'But now consider,' continued the Buddha, 'How would you feel if you heard of the kidnap of the son of the king of your neighbouring country?'

'Well of course,' said the king, 'It wouldn't affect me in the same way, I'd be sorry to hear such sad news of course, but.....'

'So you see,' concluded the Buddha, 'Suffering and unhappiness begins in love and attachment.'

We tend to complicate our lives because we can't let go. We prescribe certain rules for particular people and objects, the ones we are close to, and not for others. For those we don't care so much.

If you lose your expensive watch, my concern will not be as strong as if I had lost my watch. I might even call you careless and stupid. But the circumstances surrounding the loss of my watch I would call something else. An accident, and possibly not even my fault, and I would definitely suffer more.

Attachment and clinging.

To really progress along the spiritual path we need to simplify our life. We need to develop an honest foundation. Honesty with ourselves and our motivations, and from that, honesty with all beings. This we can only do by purifying our centre, our Spiritual Heart.

If we are to speak, we should keep our language simple. Say what we mean, and mean what we say. There is no need to enter into a long intellectual discussion, reinforcing our own particular point of view. Just say what has to be said, and let it go. And don't look for results either. From a pure centre we can always say what we feel without anticipating a response.

The simplicity and economy of words became very apparent to me one time on a boat journey from Folkstone to the Hook of Holland. I was sitting next to a young man from Morocco. We had exchanged a few words, but his English wasn't too good. He stood up, intending to go to the cafeteria, and asked me if I would like a drink.

"Oh, sure. That would be really nice. It's very kind of you. If you're sure it's not too much trouble. I can always go myself. I don't want to put you out. O.K. I'll have a tea please," I said.

He looked at me and walked away. When he returned he had brought only one drink with him. The one for himself. I realised immediately that I had said too much, and he had not understood. Instead of simply saying, 'Yes please, I'll have a cup of tea,' I had rambled on and on, and ended up confusing him.

Say what you mean, and keep it simple.

The clearest way of expressing this attitude of simplicity and honesty is with the expression, 'Always face the Dhamma'.

Dhamma is a Buddhist word that means Ultimate Truth. When our intention is always to live life by facing the Ultimate Truth, what can go wrong? Even when things don't go according to our plans, we can always be open to their teaching.

If we don't look for happiness, happiness comes by itself. But we need to be open and not attach ourselves to our fantasies and endless mental projections.

It is said that in the mind of the true spiritual practitioner there are no desires, only preferences.

This means to let go of the attachment towards our own ideas of how things should be for us, and accept everything as it is. If you desire to sleep in a comfortable bed, but the only thing available is a settee, you will be unhappy. But if you only have the preference for a comfortable bed, when the settee is offered, you will accept it graciously. Not only that, you will not hold in your mind the attraction of a bed. This is real happiness. Accepting the conditions you cannot change, and being at peace with them. Trying to sleep on a settee, whilst wishing you were in a nice comfortable bed, is just more suffering.

It is true that when we first become involved in spiritual practice there seems to be so many things about ourselves we need to change. So many different things wrong with us, that the task is endless. But the philosophy here is to 'Keep it Simple'. There is no need to change everything in our life. We just need to change one thing. From that everything else flows. By itself, with no effort involved.

But what is that one thing?

It is our heart. Our Spiritual Heart.

Let go of ego. Let go of trying to run the world and make everything perfect for you, and simply be open. Work with what you have. It is not possible to make everything right all of the time, no matter how hard you try. Understand that and turn inward.
The spiritual life isn't a secret. It's truths are all around us. No need to change anything. Just be. From that, everything changes anyway.

So how do we learn to let go of all the things we are attached to?

Think about it. How do we let go of anything?

We simply relax our grip and let them fall away. No effort

is required.   Effort is only needed to hold onto them.   All the pain, heartache and disappointment in life is caused by holding onto things that are already, by their very nature, moving away from us.   Through not letting go.

Keep it simple.   Keep everything simple.
Simplify your life by letting go of the things that hurt you. Recognise that life itself, however it manifests, is the opportunity to allow all the pain and suffering you experience, just by being alive, to fall away.

The teachings of the greatest Masters can be explained simply.   Follow their example, and discover real and lasting happiness.
The happiness of liberation.

THE EMPTY MIND

There is only one mind

THE EMPTY MIND

There were once two teachers of opposite characteristics. One kept the Buddhist precepts scrupulously, and so never drank alcohol or ate in the afternoon, whilst the other often enjoyed a drink, and ate whenever he felt like it.

One day the first teacher visited the second one, who was drinking a glass of sake.

"Hello brother," said the second teacher, "Will you have a drink?"

"I never drink," said the first teacher solemnly.

"One who does not drink is not even human," replied the second teacher.

"Do you mean to call me inhuman," exclaimed the first teacher, "Just because I will not drink alcohol? If I am not human, then please tell me exactly what I am."

"A Buddha," replied the second teacher.

Often when we embark upon a spiritual life-style we hold very high expectations of ourselves. Listening to beautiful Dhamma talks about the refined qualities of mind, and sometimes even experiencing them for ourselves, we begin to feel that this is how things should always be for us. Calm, peaceful and loving. Living in harmony with all things.

And then something happens.

A situation occurs, and we feel we've lost it.

Gone are those calm and peaceful feelings we treasured so much, and what is left is anger, resentment and even hatred. But that is not all. Also arising with these feelings is the thought, 'I shouldn't feel like this'.

Now those feelings become compounded.

At first there was just anger, but now there is anger, and guilt. Then remorse. Then the desire to feel different. Then the wish that the incident had never happened, and a sense of failure in practice. On and on it goes. Round and round. Spinning wildly in confusion and totally out of control.

In the book 'Inner Chapters', Chuang Tsu tells us that 'No Self is True Self'.
This is a very beautiful way of expressing that which cannot be expressed. The truth of our reality. That behind every movement of mind there is nothing. Only emptiness. No Self. Only the delusive attachment to our mental states as being what we are. When these mental states are noble and worthy, we feel happy, we feel we are expressing our true nature, our true self. But when these mental states are low and unworthy, we feel a sense of guilt and shame, believing these to come from our darker side. Our enemy within.
We fail to see that they all begin in the same place.
The mind.

There is only one mind. Not many.

Not the mind we want, and the mind we don't want. Not the mind we face in meditation, and the mind we take back into the world with us. Not the mind we love with, and the mind we hate with.

Only one mind, with each thought, feeling, mood and emotion emanating from the same place.

And all these thoughts, feelings, moods and emotions have the same quality. Whether they are pleasant or unpleasant, noble or low, they are all simply passing through our consciousness. Like sticks floating down a river.

Behind every passing moment of resentment, or anger or hostility, is the empty mind. The mind of No-Self. The Pure mind.

So what to do?

As always the answer is simple.

Let go. Just let go.

If anger arises, let it go. If guilt about the anger arises, let that go too. Let everything go until the purity of No-Self shines through.

One student asked his teacher, "If I haven't anything in my mind, what shall I do?"
The teacher replied, "Throw it out."
"But if I haven't anything how can I throw it out?" continued the student.
"Very well then," said the teacher, "Carry it out."

Whatever arises into your mind, let it go.
If it's not you anyway, why hold on to it? It is the very holding on to all the things that we think are ourselves that causes all our pain and suffering. Anger is not us. Guilt is not us. Resentment is not us. Happiness is not us. They are all simply movements of mind, arising because of conditions. If we can recognise them for what they are, and let them go, they have no power over us. The more we can let go, the more peaceful our lives become.

One meditation Master has said, 'Let go a little, and there is a little peace. Let go a lot, and there is a lot of peace.

Let go completely, and there is complete peace.'

Complete peace arising from an empty mind. A mind free from the attachment and delusion that these things are what we are.

There is nothing that we are really, and no way we need to be. Practice letting go until there is no more to let go of, and be free.

LIVING IN THE SUNSHINE

**People are the way they are, that is their choice.
You are the way you are, that is your choice**

LIVING IN THE SUNSHINE

A feudal lord once asked a Zen Master how he might pass the time. He felt his days to be very long attending his office, and sitting stiffly to receive the homage of others. The Zen Master wrote eight Chinese characters on a piece of paper and gave them to the lord. The characters read;

This day will not come again,
Each minute is worth a priceless gem.

A modern spiritual teacher has said that there are only two ways to live, the right way and the wrong way. This is the choice that faces all of us. How do you want to live?

The wrong way is the most popular choice. Seeing life as a series of problems to be resolved, as a struggle against all the misfortune that can befall a person. Creating an ideal scenario in our mind of how things should be for us. A mental Utopia, and then working as hard as possible to make it happen.

We carry memories from the past, and then compare our present and future to them. 'Was I happier then? Will I be that happy again?' We continually repeat the same formulas for personal happiness, and when they fail to fully satisfy us, we simply start again. Mistakes made in the past are repeated over and over. And our quest is always the same. Personal happiness, a sense of well being and a pleasant life. We fall into the trap of believing, 'If only I had that, I'd be happy', or 'If only I didn't have this, I'd be happy'. Happiness is always seen as the goal of the future, something we have to work toward. 'I'm not happy now, but in ten years, if all goes well, I will be'.

Because of this very projection we miss the moment. We

miss the possibility of now.

In reality there is no time other than now. The past is just a memory, and the future is just an idea, and when do we experience the past and the future? Now, right now, and at no other time.

Every memory that arises within you is experienced as a thought, now. Every future plan that arises within you is experienced as a thought, now. There is no time other than now. Everything else is imagination.

When I was teaching in India, in the small town of Budh Gaya, the place of the Buddhas enlightenment, I would often visit the Stupa that marks the spot, early in the morning.

My reason for doing this, as with most visitors to the area, was to perform 'Kora', or circumambulation of the shrine. This is to walk in meditation around the main object of veneration, the Bodhi Tree, and the surrounding area.

Because the Stupa, which is something like a small religious park, is walled, the rising sun shines directly on to one part, and only partially onto the other. I noticed that each time I reached the shaded area, I would cross over into the sunshine again, and therefore perform the whole of my 'Kora', taking about one hour, enjoying the light and warmth of the sun.

It's no secret that the sun has a pleasant effect upon us, and generally makes everyone feel better. It's the winter we dread, never the summer. For most people the summer cannot come quickly enough, and usually passes too soon. For me in Budh Gaya, to come out of the shade into the sunshine was a natural response. I did it without giving it a second thought. It was a spontaneous action.

As I continued to walk, I began to reflect upon this action.

NO-ONE CAN DO IT FOR YOU

There was once a Japanese wrestler who was immensely strong and talented. In private bouts he defeated even his own teacher. However, in public it was a different matter. Even the most inexperienced of opponents could throw him easily. Naturally he was very concerned by this, and so he sought the help of a Zen Master.

"Your name is O Nami, Great Waves," said the Zen Master, "So tonight I want you to stay in this temple and meditate. Imagine you are those sweeping billows. You are no longer a wrestler who is afraid. You are those huge waves washing away everything before you. Do this and you will become the greatest wrestler in the land."

O Nami did as he was asked. As the night progressed he imagined himself first as ripples, and then building up power, becoming bigger and stronger. In his mind he was washing away everything in sight. Even the statue of the Buddha was not safe from his power.

In the morning the Zen Master returned to find O Nami still deep in meditation, with a faint smile on his face. He patted the wrestler's shoulder and said, "Now nothing can disturb you. You are those great waves you were named after. You will sweep away everything before you."

The same day O Nami entered the wrestling contests and won. After that no-one was able to defeat him.

Meditation is a powerful force in our lives. With it we can change everything about the way we live. However, like O Nami in the story, even with the help of a Zen Master, the work that had to be done, he had to do by himself. Even with expert guidance, he was alone. It was just him and his mind.

There are many stories of Gurus, dynamic and powerful teachers, who, with only a touch, are able to enlighten others. Spiritual seekers are often impressed by such stories, and will expend a great deal of time and effort locating a teacher with this kind of reputation just to be touched by them, and spend time in their presence. However, whatever they may believe happens in such contact, what definitely does not happen is the eradication of their delusion and ignorance. This cannot be done by another. It has to be done by ourselves.

The Buddha taught for forty five years after his enlightenment. It was his wish that as many people as possible would benefit from his teaching and attain enlightenment. He would have liked to end all the suffering in the world and see everyone as him, enlightened. If this could have been done with just a touch, to be sure, he would have done it.
But the Buddha said that, 'No-one can purify another. Purity and impurity are solely personal concerns'.
Jesus also taught in the same way. He said that 'No-one can enter the Kingdom of Heaven except through me'. Even though the Kingdom of Heaven is on offer, the approach has to be made by each one of us individually. No-one can go for us.

Meditation is the key to self purity, and to entering the Kingdom of Heaven. There is no difference between the two. Once we have removed greed, hatred and delusion from our mind, the manifestation of ignorance, we are already in the Kingdom of Heaven. We don't have to wait until we are dead. We can do it now.
Of course, in spiritual training we need a teacher, someone who can show us the way, and explain to us the simplicity of practice. But as always, this is all they can do. Point,

instruct, and possibly even bully us into practice, but they cannot do the practice for us. This is the one thing we have to do for ourselves.

In meditation we face ourselves. We face our past. All our memories and conditioning rise up to confront us, and we have to sit quietly and let it pass. Painful or pleasant, good or bad, we have to let it go. This activity we have to do alone. Once in meditation we are by ourselves, facing ourselves. This is why we need to be brave and prepared to go deep. To penetrate all the delusions we hold about ourselves and the world.

Many non meditators think of meditation as an escape from the world, a settling back into a quiet and peaceful environment, and giving up on real life. Nothing could be further from the truth. Meditation is a true facing of the world. Our world. The one we create with our thoughts and feelings, and the one we most definitely live in. In meditation we don't look at others, and we don't follow someone elses breathing pattern. We turn to our own breath, and allow everything else to fall away.

This is such a beautiful practice, and is ultimately the only thing that will lead to Insight. The practice of Awareness. We take this attitude of careful watching, of witnessing our own mind and its reactions into everyday life with us, not confining it to formal meditation practice only, but applying it to all situations. We are alone in meditation, and we are alone in life. There is just us, responsible for all the pain and unhappiness we experience.

No-one else is to blame. We do it to ourselves.

Many people complain that after the initial blissful

experiences of a newly started awareness practice, their meditation becomes busy and confused as they are bombarded by thoughts and feelings that are completely unexpected. Gone is the peace of those earlier sittings, and now arising is the desire to get back to the way it used to be.

However contrary it may seem, in actual fact, this is a good sign. The past being released into the present, that we can face without either suppression or indulgence. The process of purification.

This is like the story of the man who wanted to leave the town he had always lived in.

This particular man had grown up in his home town. He had married, raised a family and gone into business. In order to do this he had borrowed a lot of money. One day the man decided to leave this town behind him, and begin a new life elsewhere. But before he could do this he had to pay back all his debts. Everything he had borrowed in the past had to be repaid.

This is exactly how it is for us in our meditation. Repaying all the debts of the past. No-one can do this for us. They are our debts, and only we can repay them. Personally. This is the ultimate teaching in spiritual practice. We are always by ourselves, reaping the results of the past.

There are many Gurus in the world, with a great many powers, but in truth, the greatest power belongs to us. The ability to let the past go, and be completely free from its influence.

This is how the greatest Masters teach. Showing us that our development is within our own hands only. No-one can do it for us. Only we can set ourselves free.

Don't miss this opportunity. The chance to change your life is right here, right now. Only you can do it.

HIGHER THAN HAPPINESS

**There is a way we can live that is in fact,
higher than happiness**

HIGHER THAN HAPPINESS

'I just keep doing the practice, and everything seems to work out very well.'

Michael Kewley in answer to a question.

As human beings our common goal is the same. It doesn't matter if we are Easterners or Westerners, highly intelligent and sophisticated, or completely stupid. It doesn't matter where we live either. In a village in the Brazilian jungle, or in a modern city in the so called 'first world'. We all want the same. And what we want is to be happy.

Actually, this is not such an unreasonable request is it? We are born into this world and at some point, usually quite early, experience unhappiness, and we don't like it. It doesn't feel good. Perhaps just as a baby, when we're too hot, or to cold, or we want feeding or changing, we experience feelings of discomfort and we react. We want to change our present situation for something more favourable. As we grow and develop mentally we become much more subtle as to our demands. We hold the concept of happiness within us, and then try to arrange everything contained in our sphere of control to promote that concept. Perhaps now we don't simply cry out for conditions to change as we did when we were babies, but apart from that, everything is the same. We know what we want, and if we don't get it, we suffer.

Happiness is very illusive. It comes and goes by itself. There is nothing any of us can do to determine its arising, and nothing we can do to make it stay once it appears. This is the nature of happiness. It comes and goes due to conditions. It is completely impersonal.

Of course, happiness is real.

We can say it's vague and difficult to define, but we all know what it feels like. It feels pleasant, and that is what we want. A life filled with only pleasant feelings. No-one enjoys the opposites of happiness. Depression, frustration, irritation and the rest. These are the feelings we try to keep away. It is a constant battle each day. The feelings we want contrasted to the feelings we don't want.

So how do we attempt to promote the feelings we want? By turning outwards into the material, emotional and spiritual world. By organising the different aspects of life so that we are never unhappy.

But of course it doesn't work, does it?

Each time we acquire a new material possession we feel happy. The new video recorder, or washing machine, or car, or house, or anything at all, we experience a happy feeling. In this sense happiness is real. But this feeling of happiness doesn't last. It has no sustaining power. Soon it passes, and although we may have a new material possession, it just becomes one more thing to worry about, or keep in good repair, or simply carry around with us. In reality it just becomes a burden.

In the emotional life we need people to love and care for us so that we can be happy. How often have we met the man or woman of our dreams, only to find that they fail us in some way? They are not the people who can make us happy all the time.
Families are the same. Our parents, children, brothers and sisters, fail to meet our expectations of them, and again we suffer. We feel let down and disappointed. Our hopes for

happiness through them dashed.

The spiritual life is no different. By turning outwards to a new religion or system of living we feel we can be happy. Initially, as with the material and emotional world, this can be true, but unless we investigate the inherent nature of happiness, this too will fail us.
A new religion can be like a new car. At first it brings happiness, but when things begin to go wrong, it just becomes another burden.
Perhaps then we feel a change is in order, and so we look for something else. Something that will bring back that feeling of happiness.

Actually, happiness is not the problem.

It is our attachment to it that creates our suffering and dissatisfaction.
It is time now to turn away from looking outside ourselves for happiness, and understand where happiness truly begins and ends.

The Buddha understood this clearly when he was living as a prince in his father's palace. Even though he had, and could have, anything he wanted, he was still not happy all the time. He would be faced with boredom, frustration and disappointment, just like the poorest beggars outside the palace walls. Even when we have everything we think we want, we cannot determine the arising of happiness.

So what can we do?

There is a way we can live that is in fact, higher than happiness.

Through the practice of Insight Meditation we examine the very source of our unhappiness and the desire to change the situation we find ourselves in. Through the constant determination of recognising all of our thoughts, feelings, moods and emotions as 'not me, not mine, not what I am', we release ourselves from their grasp.

This is not magic. This is not a special technique available to adherents of only a certain religion. This is the potential for all human beings. To understand the mind and body as they truly are. 'Not me, not mine, not what I am'. As this understanding begins to grow through practice, the simplistic desire for happiness, and the insistence that everyone and everything conduct themselves according to our view so that we may experience that happiness, falls away. By no longer trying to control the universe to suit our demand, but allowing everything to be, we experience peace.

No more struggle. No more fight. No more suffering.

Surrendering into this state we experience the mind that is indeed, higher than happiness. We benefit, all beings benefit. We no longer add to the general confusion of the world, as one more ego just wanting its own way, but we abide peacefully, knowing when to speak and when to keep quiet. When to act, and when to be still.

This is such a wonderful practice. The way of effortless effort. Of knowing things as they really are.

The Japanese Zen Buddhists say this very beautifully in the verse:

Sitting quietly, doing nothing,
Spring comes,
And the grass grows by itself.

Sitting quietly doing nothing, is the meditation practice. Not trying to control the mind, but being at peace with it. The pleasant and the unpleasant. Realising that thoughts, moods, feelings and emotions come and go without end. If this is their nature, why try to hold on to some at the expense of others? Let them go. Let them all go.

Spring comes, is the result of this practice. The peace and understanding that arises out of it. It is the fruit of our effort.

And the grass grows by itself, is the effect this practice has on our lives. Not confining itself to formal meditation sittings, but radiating outwards from our heart to affect the way we live in the world. Moment by moment.

There is nothing extra you need to do. There is nowhere you need to be. Everything is right here for you right now. Turn to yourself and begin to experience a way of living that is beyond the selfish and immature demands to be happy, and realise a life that is indeed, higher than happiness.

MICHAEL KEWLEY

Dhamma Teacher

Michael Kewley is a modern spiritual teacher. In Nineteen Seventy One, at the age of twenty, he stumbled into the Transcendental system of meditation, as taught by the Maharishi Mahesh Yogi, and for the next twenty years devoted himself to a life of spiritual pursuit. Practising with many different teachers from different spiritual backgrounds, he developed his meditation skills, and the moral requirements demanded by the true devotee. In nineteen eighty seven he ordained as a short term Buddhist monk under the watchful eye of his senior teacher, Sayadaw Rewata Dhamma, a Burmese abbot and meditation master of international repute.

On the express instruction of the Sayadaw he began to teach meditation and spiritual practice, establishing a flourishing group on his native Isle of Man. Many meditation retreats, workshops, seminars and instruction courses later, he left to visit India.

On a four month pilgrimage to the Buddhist holy places, he found himself teaching many Westerners in the small town of Budh Gaya, the place of the Buddhas enlightenment. This led to an invitation from the International Meditation Centre there to remain as senior European instructor. Michael declined the offer, but returns each year for two months to lead intensive meditation retreats.

Michael also teaches Insight and Loving Kindness Meditation throughout Europe and the United Kingdom, but still resides in the Isle of Man.

Also by
Michael Kewley

The Panna Dipa Home Meditation Course
A five-week structured and guided course
of Insight and Loving Kindness Meditation.
Course book plus three cassettes.

Teaching from the Spiritual Heart
Build on course
for the Panna Dipa Home Meditation Course.
Course book plus two cassettes.

For information concerning
Courses, Seminars, Retreats and Workshops
please contact:

Panna Dipa Meditation Centre
6 Brighton Terrace
Douglas
Isle of Man, IM1 4AP
U.K.

Tel: 01624 612819

Notes